50 Great Canadian BBQ Recipes

By: Kelly Johnson

Table of Contents

- Maple-Glazed BBQ Salmon
- Cedar-Planked Atlantic Salmon
- Grilled Alberta Beef Steaks
- BBQ Maple Pork Chops
- Smoked Brisket with Canadian Dry Rub
- Grilled Bison Burgers
- BBQ Moose Ribs
- Montreal-Style Smoked Meat Sandwich
- Maple Whiskey BBQ Chicken
- Grilled Lobster Tails with Garlic Butter
- BBQ Poutine with Smoked Meat
- Grilled Wild Boar Sausages
- Smoked Duck Breast with Maple Glaze
- BBQ Peameal Bacon on a Bun
- Honey-Mustard Grilled Chicken
- Grilled Venison Steaks
- BBQ Butterflied Trout
- Smoked Maple Beans
- BBQ Corn on the Cob with Herb Butter
- Cedar-Smoked Arctic Char
- Grilled Elk Medallions
- Smoked Pulled Pork with Maple BBQ Sauce
- BBQ Bison Short Ribs
- Grilled Maple-Glazed Pineapple
- Canadian Cheddar-Stuffed Burgers
- BBQ Shrimp Skewers with Maple Chili Glaze
- Honey-Garlic BBQ Chicken Wings
- Smoked Gouda and Bacon Burgers
- BBQ Trout Tacos with Slaw
- Montreal Spice-Rubbed BBQ Chicken
- Grilled Halibut with Lemon Butter
- Smoked Turkey Drumsticks
- BBQ Duck Breast with Blueberry Sauce
- Maple-Chipotle BBQ Ribs
- Grilled Wild Mushroom Skewers

- BBQ Buffalo Chicken Poutine
- Campfire BBQ Bannock
- Smoked Salmon on Cedar Plank
- BBQ Glazed Root Vegetables
- Grilled Peppers and Zucchini with Maple Drizzle
- Smoked Maple Bacon-Wrapped Scallops
- BBQ Pork Belly Burnt Ends
- Grilled Lamb Chops with Rosemary Maple Glaze
- BBQ Chicken Drumsticks with Hickory Sauce
- Grilled Peach and Brie Crostini
- Maple-Smoked Sausage Links
- BBQ S'mores with Maple Graham Crackers
- Smoked Arctic Char Tacos
- Grilled Sweet Potatoes with Maple Butter
- BBQ Pulled Moose Sliders

Maple-Glazed BBQ Salmon

Ingredients

- 1 lb salmon fillet
- 1/4 cup maple syrup
- 2 tbsp Dijon mustard
- 1 tbsp soy sauce
- 1 tsp garlic powder
- 1/2 tsp black pepper

Instructions

1. Preheat grill to medium heat.
2. Mix maple syrup, mustard, soy sauce, garlic powder, and black pepper.
3. Brush glaze over salmon and grill for 4-5 minutes per side, basting occasionally.

Cedar-Planked Atlantic Salmon

Ingredients

- 1 salmon fillet (about 1.5 lbs)
- 1 cedar plank, soaked for 1 hour
- 1/4 cup maple syrup
- 1 tbsp Dijon mustard
- 1 tbsp olive oil
- 1 tsp thyme
- 1/2 tsp salt

Instructions

1. Preheat grill to medium heat.
2. Mix maple syrup, mustard, olive oil, thyme, and salt.
3. Place salmon on the cedar plank and brush with the glaze.
4. Grill with the lid closed for 15-20 minutes.

Grilled Alberta Beef Steaks

Ingredients

- 2 Alberta beef ribeye steaks
- 2 tbsp olive oil
- 1 tbsp Montreal steak seasoning
- 1 tsp garlic powder
- 1/2 tsp black pepper

Instructions

1. Preheat grill to high heat.
2. Rub steaks with olive oil and season with spices.
3. Grill for 4-5 minutes per side for medium-rare.
4. Let rest for 5 minutes before serving.

BBQ Maple Pork Chops

Ingredients

- 4 pork chops
- 1/4 cup maple syrup
- 2 tbsp soy sauce
- 1 tbsp apple cider vinegar
- 1/2 tsp smoked paprika
- 1/2 tsp black pepper

Instructions

1. Preheat grill to medium-high heat.
2. Mix maple syrup, soy sauce, vinegar, paprika, and pepper.
3. Marinate pork chops for at least 1 hour.
4. Grill for 4-5 minutes per side, basting with extra glaze.

Smoked Brisket with Canadian Dry Rub

Ingredients

- 4 lb brisket
- 2 tbsp smoked paprika
- 1 tbsp kosher salt
- 1 tbsp black pepper
- 1 tbsp brown sugar
- 1 tsp garlic powder
- 1 tsp onion powder
- 1/2 tsp cayenne pepper

Instructions

1. Rub brisket with dry seasoning and let sit overnight.
2. Preheat smoker to 225°F (110°C).
3. Smoke for 8-10 hours, until tender, wrapping in foil halfway through.

Grilled Bison Burgers

Ingredients

- 1 lb ground bison
- 1/4 cup breadcrumbs
- 1 egg
- 1 tsp Worcestershire sauce
- 1/2 tsp salt
- 1/4 tsp black pepper

Instructions

1. Mix all ingredients and form into patties.
2. Preheat grill to medium-high heat.
3. Cook burgers for 4-5 minutes per side.

BBQ Moose Ribs

Ingredients

- 2 lbs moose ribs
- 1/2 cup maple syrup
- 1/4 cup apple cider vinegar
- 1/4 cup ketchup
- 1 tbsp Worcestershire sauce
- 1 tsp smoked paprika
- 1/2 tsp salt

Instructions

1. Preheat grill to low heat.
2. Mix maple syrup, vinegar, ketchup, Worcestershire sauce, paprika, and salt.
3. Baste ribs with sauce and grill for 2 hours, turning occasionally.

Montreal-Style Smoked Meat Sandwich

Ingredients

- 1 lb Montreal smoked meat, sliced
- 4 rye bread slices
- 2 tbsp yellow mustard

Instructions

1. Warm the smoked meat by steaming for 10 minutes.
2. Spread mustard on rye bread.
3. Pile high with smoked meat and serve warm.

Maple Whiskey BBQ Chicken

Ingredients

- 1 whole chicken, cut into pieces
- 1/4 cup maple syrup
- 1/4 cup whiskey
- 2 tbsp Dijon mustard
- 1 tbsp apple cider vinegar
- 1 tsp smoked paprika
- 1/2 tsp salt

Instructions

1. Mix maple syrup, whiskey, mustard, vinegar, paprika, and salt.
2. Marinate chicken for at least 2 hours.
3. Grill over medium heat for 30-35 minutes, basting with sauce.

Grilled Lobster Tails with Garlic Butter

Ingredients

- 4 lobster tails
- 1/4 cup butter, melted
- 2 cloves garlic, minced
- 1 tbsp lemon juice
- 1/2 tsp paprika
- 1/2 tsp salt
- 1/4 tsp black pepper

Instructions

1. Preheat grill to medium-high heat.
2. Cut lobster tails in half lengthwise.
3. Mix melted butter, garlic, lemon juice, paprika, salt, and pepper.
4. Brush lobster tails with garlic butter and grill for 5-6 minutes, basting frequently.

BBQ Poutine with Smoked Meat

Ingredients

- 4 cups French fries, cooked
- 1 cup cheese curds
- 1/2 cup smoked meat, sliced
- 1 cup BBQ gravy

Instructions

1. Place fries on a serving dish.
2. Sprinkle cheese curds and smoked meat on top.
3. Pour hot BBQ gravy over everything and serve immediately.

Grilled Wild Boar Sausages

Ingredients

- 4 wild boar sausages
- 1 tbsp olive oil
- 1/2 tsp black pepper
- 1/2 tsp smoked paprika

Instructions

1. Preheat grill to medium heat.
2. Lightly brush sausages with olive oil and season with pepper and paprika.
3. Grill for 6-8 minutes, turning occasionally.

Smoked Duck Breast with Maple Glaze

Ingredients

- 2 duck breasts
- 1/4 cup maple syrup
- 1 tbsp soy sauce
- 1 tsp Dijon mustard
- 1/2 tsp black pepper

Instructions

1. Score the duck skin and season with black pepper.
2. Smoke at 225°F (110°C) for 1.5 hours.
3. Mix maple syrup, soy sauce, and mustard, then brush over duck.
4. Sear skin-side down in a hot pan until crispy.

BBQ Peameal Bacon on a Bun

Ingredients

- 4 slices peameal bacon
- 4 sandwich buns
- 2 tbsp Dijon mustard
- 2 tbsp maple syrup

Instructions

1. Preheat grill to medium heat.
2. Brush peameal bacon with maple syrup and grill for 4-5 minutes per side.
3. Serve on buns with Dijon mustard.

Honey-Mustard Grilled Chicken

Ingredients

- 4 chicken breasts
- 1/4 cup honey
- 2 tbsp Dijon mustard
- 1 tbsp olive oil
- 1/2 tsp salt
- 1/4 tsp black pepper

Instructions

1. Mix honey, mustard, olive oil, salt, and pepper.
2. Marinate chicken for at least 1 hour.
3. Grill over medium heat for 6-7 minutes per side.

Grilled Venison Steaks

Ingredients

- 2 venison steaks
- 2 tbsp olive oil
- 1 tbsp Worcestershire sauce
- 1 tsp garlic powder
- 1/2 tsp black pepper
- 1/2 tsp salt

Instructions

1. Marinate venison steaks in olive oil, Worcestershire sauce, garlic powder, salt, and pepper for 2 hours.
2. Preheat grill to high heat.
3. Grill steaks for 4-5 minutes per side for medium-rare.

BBQ Butterflied Trout

Ingredients

- 1 whole trout, butterflied
- 2 tbsp olive oil
- 1 tbsp lemon juice
- 2 cloves garlic, minced
- 1/2 tsp salt
- 1/4 tsp black pepper

Instructions

1. Preheat grill to medium heat.
2. Brush trout with olive oil, lemon juice, garlic, salt, and pepper.
3. Grill skin-side down for 5-7 minutes.

Smoked Maple Beans

Ingredients

- 2 cups navy beans, soaked overnight
- 1/2 cup maple syrup
- 1/4 cup molasses
- 1/2 cup bacon, chopped
- 1 small onion, chopped
- 4 cups water
- 1/2 tsp mustard powder
- 1/2 tsp salt

Instructions

1. Preheat smoker to 250°F (120°C).
2. Mix beans, maple syrup, molasses, bacon, onion, water, mustard, and salt in a baking dish.
3. Smoke for 4-5 hours, stirring occasionally.

BBQ Corn on the Cob with Herb Butter

Ingredients

- 4 ears corn, husked
- 1/4 cup butter, softened
- 1 tbsp fresh parsley, chopped
- 1 tsp garlic powder
- 1/2 tsp salt
- 1/4 tsp black pepper

Instructions

1. Preheat grill to medium heat.
2. Mix butter, parsley, garlic powder, salt, and pepper.
3. Brush corn with herb butter and wrap in foil.
4. Grill for 15-20 minutes, turning occasionally.

Cedar-Smoked Arctic Char

Ingredients

- 2 Arctic char fillets
- 1 cedar plank, soaked for 1 hour
- 1/4 cup maple syrup
- 1 tbsp Dijon mustard
- 1 tbsp olive oil
- 1/2 tsp salt
- 1/2 tsp black pepper

Instructions

1. Preheat grill to medium heat.
2. Mix maple syrup, mustard, olive oil, salt, and pepper.
3. Place fish on cedar plank and brush with glaze.
4. Grill for 15-20 minutes with the lid closed.

Grilled Elk Medallions

Ingredients

- 4 elk medallions
- 2 tbsp olive oil
- 1 tbsp Worcestershire sauce
- 1 tsp garlic powder
- 1/2 tsp black pepper
- 1/2 tsp salt

Instructions

1. Marinate elk medallions in olive oil, Worcestershire sauce, garlic powder, salt, and pepper for 1 hour.
2. Preheat grill to high heat.
3. Grill for 3-4 minutes per side for medium-rare.

Smoked Pulled Pork with Maple BBQ Sauce

Ingredients

- 4 lb pork shoulder
- 2 tbsp paprika
- 1 tbsp garlic powder
- 1 tbsp black pepper
- 1 tbsp salt
- 1/2 tsp cayenne pepper

Maple BBQ Sauce

- 1/2 cup maple syrup
- 1 cup ketchup
- 2 tbsp apple cider vinegar
- 1 tbsp Worcestershire sauce
- 1/2 tsp smoked paprika

Instructions

1. Rub pork with seasoning and let sit for 1 hour.
2. Smoke at 225°F (110°C) for 8-10 hours until tender.
3. Mix sauce ingredients in a saucepan and simmer for 10 minutes.
4. Shred pork and mix with sauce.

BBQ Bison Short Ribs

Ingredients

- 2 lbs bison short ribs
- 1/4 cup maple syrup
- 1/4 cup apple cider vinegar
- 1/4 cup soy sauce
- 2 cloves garlic, minced
- 1/2 tsp black pepper

Instructions

1. Preheat grill to low heat.
2. Mix maple syrup, vinegar, soy sauce, garlic, and pepper.
3. Marinate ribs for at least 4 hours.
4. Grill over low heat for 2-3 hours, basting with marinade.

Grilled Maple-Glazed Pineapple

Ingredients

- 1 pineapple, peeled and sliced
- 1/4 cup maple syrup
- 1 tsp cinnamon

Instructions

1. Preheat grill to medium heat.
2. Brush pineapple slices with maple syrup and sprinkle with cinnamon.
3. Grill for 2-3 minutes per side.

Canadian Cheddar-Stuffed Burgers

Ingredients

- 1 lb ground beef
- 1/2 cup Canadian cheddar, cubed
- 1 tsp Worcestershire sauce
- 1/2 tsp salt
- 1/2 tsp black pepper

Instructions

1. Mix beef, Worcestershire sauce, salt, and pepper.
2. Shape into patties, placing a cheddar cube inside each.
3. Grill over medium heat for 4-5 minutes per side.

BBQ Shrimp Skewers with Maple Chili Glaze

Ingredients

- 1 lb shrimp, peeled and deveined
- 1/4 cup maple syrup
- 1 tbsp soy sauce
- 1 tsp chili flakes
- 1/2 tsp garlic powder
- Wooden skewers, soaked

Instructions

1. Preheat grill to medium-high heat.
2. Mix maple syrup, soy sauce, chili flakes, and garlic powder.
3. Thread shrimp onto skewers and brush with glaze.
4. Grill for 2-3 minutes per side.

Honey-Garlic BBQ Chicken Wings

Ingredients

- 2 lbs chicken wings
- 1/4 cup honey
- 2 tbsp soy sauce
- 2 cloves garlic, minced
- 1/2 tsp black pepper

Instructions

1. Preheat grill to medium heat.
2. Mix honey, soy sauce, garlic, and pepper.
3. Marinate wings for at least 1 hour.
4. Grill for 6-8 minutes per side.

Smoked Gouda and Bacon Burgers

Ingredients

- 1 lb ground beef
- 1/2 cup smoked Gouda, cubed
- 4 slices bacon, cooked and crumbled
- 1 tsp Worcestershire sauce
- 1/2 tsp salt
- 1/2 tsp black pepper

Instructions

1. Mix beef, Worcestershire sauce, salt, and pepper.
2. Shape into patties, stuffing Gouda and bacon inside.
3. Grill over medium heat for 4-5 minutes per side.

BBQ Trout Tacos with Slaw

Ingredients

- 2 trout fillets
- 1 tbsp olive oil
- 1 tsp smoked paprika
- 1/2 tsp cumin
- 1/2 tsp salt
- 1/4 tsp black pepper
- 8 small tortillas

Slaw

- 2 cups cabbage, shredded
- 1/4 cup carrots, shredded
- 2 tbsp lime juice
- 1 tbsp maple syrup
- 1/4 tsp salt

Instructions

1. Preheat grill to medium heat.
2. Rub trout with olive oil, paprika, cumin, salt, and pepper.
3. Grill skin-side down for 4-5 minutes.
4. Mix slaw ingredients and set aside.
5. Flake trout into tortillas and top with slaw.

Montreal Spice-Rubbed BBQ Chicken

Ingredients

- 4 chicken thighs
- 2 tbsp Montreal steak spice
- 1 tbsp olive oil
- 1 tbsp maple syrup

Instructions

1. Preheat grill to medium-high heat.
2. Rub chicken with olive oil, Montreal spice, and maple syrup.
3. Grill for 5-6 minutes per side.

Grilled Halibut with Lemon Butter

Ingredients

- 2 halibut fillets
- 2 tbsp butter, melted
- 1 tbsp lemon juice
- 1 tsp garlic powder
- 1/2 tsp salt
- 1/4 tsp black pepper

Instructions

1. Preheat grill to medium heat.
2. Brush halibut with butter, lemon juice, garlic powder, salt, and pepper.
3. Grill for 4-5 minutes per side.

Smoked Turkey Drumsticks

Ingredients

- 4 turkey drumsticks
- 2 tbsp paprika
- 1 tbsp salt
- 1 tbsp garlic powder
- 1/2 tsp black pepper
- 1/2 cup apple juice

Instructions

1. Preheat smoker to 250°F (120°C).
2. Rub turkey with seasoning.
3. Smoke for 3-4 hours, basting with apple juice.

BBQ Duck Breast with Blueberry Sauce

Ingredients

- 2 duck breasts
- 1/2 tsp salt
- 1/2 tsp black pepper
- 1/4 cup blueberries
- 1/4 cup maple syrup
- 1 tbsp balsamic vinegar

Instructions

1. Score duck skin and season with salt and pepper.
2. Grill over medium heat, skin-side down, for 6 minutes, then flip and cook for 4 minutes.
3. Simmer blueberries, maple syrup, and vinegar until thickened.
4. Drizzle sauce over grilled duck.

Maple-Chipotle BBQ Ribs

Ingredients

- 2 racks pork ribs
- 1/4 cup maple syrup
- 1/4 cup apple cider vinegar
- 1 tbsp chipotle powder
- 1 tbsp garlic powder
- 1 tsp salt

Instructions

1. Preheat grill to low heat.
2. Rub ribs with chipotle, garlic powder, and salt.
3. Grill for 3 hours, basting with maple syrup and vinegar every 30 minutes.

Grilled Wild Mushroom Skewers

Ingredients

- 2 cups wild mushrooms (chanterelles, portobello, cremini)
- 2 tbsp olive oil
- 1 tbsp balsamic vinegar
- 1/2 tsp salt
- 1/4 tsp black pepper
- Wooden skewers, soaked

Instructions

1. Preheat grill to medium heat.
2. Toss mushrooms with olive oil, vinegar, salt, and pepper.
3. Thread onto skewers and grill for 5 minutes per side.

BBQ Buffalo Chicken Poutine

Ingredients

- 2 cups French fries, cooked
- 1 cup cheese curds
- 1/2 cup cooked shredded buffalo chicken
- 1 cup gravy

Instructions

1. Arrange fries on a plate and top with cheese curds and buffalo chicken.
2. Pour hot gravy over everything and serve.

Campfire BBQ Bannock

Ingredients

- 2 cups flour
- 1 tbsp baking powder
- 1/2 tsp salt
- 1/4 cup butter, melted
- 3/4 cup water

Instructions

1. Mix flour, baking powder, and salt in a bowl.
2. Stir in melted butter and water to form a dough.
3. Shape into rounds and grill over a campfire for 10 minutes per side.

Smoked Salmon on Cedar Plank

Ingredients

- 1 salmon fillet
- 1 cedar plank, soaked for 1 hour
- 1/4 cup maple syrup
- 1 tbsp Dijon mustard
- 1 tsp garlic powder
- 1/2 tsp salt

Instructions

1. Preheat grill to medium heat.
2. Mix maple syrup, mustard, garlic powder, and salt.
3. Place salmon on cedar plank and brush with glaze.
4. Grill for 15-20 minutes.

BBQ Glazed Root Vegetables

Ingredients

- 2 cups carrots, parsnips, and sweet potatoes, chopped
- 2 tbsp olive oil
- 1/4 cup maple syrup
- 1 tbsp balsamic vinegar
- 1/2 tsp salt
- 1/2 tsp black pepper

Instructions

1. Preheat grill to medium heat.
2. Toss vegetables with olive oil, maple syrup, balsamic vinegar, salt, and pepper.
3. Grill in a grill basket for 15-20 minutes, stirring occasionally.

Grilled Peppers and Zucchini with Maple Drizzle

Ingredients

- 1 red bell pepper, sliced
- 1 yellow bell pepper, sliced
- 1 zucchini, sliced lengthwise
- 2 tbsp olive oil
- 1 tbsp maple syrup
- 1/2 tsp salt
- 1/4 tsp black pepper

Instructions

1. Preheat grill to medium-high heat.
2. Toss peppers and zucchini with olive oil, salt, and pepper.
3. Grill for 3-4 minutes per side until slightly charred.
4. Drizzle with maple syrup before serving.

Smoked Maple Bacon-Wrapped Scallops

Ingredients

- 12 large scallops
- 6 slices bacon, cut in half
- 1/4 cup maple syrup
- 1/2 tsp black pepper
- Wooden skewers, soaked

Instructions

1. Preheat smoker to 225°F (110°C).
2. Wrap each scallop with bacon and secure with a skewer.
3. Brush with maple syrup and season with black pepper.
4. Smoke for 45-60 minutes until scallops are cooked through and bacon is crisp.

BBQ Pork Belly Burnt Ends

Ingredients

- 2 lbs pork belly, cut into 1-inch cubes
- 1/4 cup BBQ rub
- 1/2 cup maple BBQ sauce
- 2 tbsp butter, melted
- 1 tbsp honey

Instructions

1. Preheat smoker to 250°F (120°C).
2. Toss pork belly cubes in BBQ rub and smoke for 2.5 hours.
3. Transfer to a foil pan, add BBQ sauce, butter, and honey, then cover and smoke for another 1.5 hours.

Grilled Lamb Chops with Rosemary Maple Glaze

Ingredients

- 4 lamb chops
- 2 tbsp olive oil
- 1/4 cup maple syrup
- 1 tbsp Dijon mustard
- 1 tbsp fresh rosemary, chopped
- 1/2 tsp salt
- 1/2 tsp black pepper

Instructions

1. Preheat grill to medium-high heat.
2. Mix maple syrup, mustard, rosemary, salt, and pepper.
3. Brush glaze on lamb chops and grill for 3-4 minutes per side.

BBQ Chicken Drumsticks with Hickory Sauce

Ingredients

- 8 chicken drumsticks
- 1/2 cup hickory BBQ sauce
- 2 tbsp maple syrup
- 1 tbsp apple cider vinegar
- 1 tsp smoked paprika
- 1/2 tsp garlic powder
- 1/2 tsp salt

Instructions

1. Preheat grill to medium heat.
2. Mix BBQ sauce, maple syrup, vinegar, paprika, garlic powder, and salt.
3. Grill drumsticks for 25-30 minutes, turning occasionally and basting with sauce.

Grilled Peach and Brie Crostini

Ingredients

- 1 baguette, sliced
- 2 ripe peaches, sliced
- 4 oz Brie cheese, sliced
- 2 tbsp maple syrup
- 1 tbsp olive oil
- 1/2 tsp black pepper

Instructions

1. Preheat grill to medium-high heat.
2. Brush baguette slices with olive oil and grill for 1-2 minutes per side.
3. Grill peach slices for 2 minutes per side.
4. Top crostini with Brie, grilled peaches, a drizzle of maple syrup, and black pepper.

Maple-Smoked Sausage Links

Ingredients

- 1 lb pork or moose sausage links
- 1/4 cup maple syrup
- 1 tbsp Dijon mustard
- 1/2 tsp black pepper

Instructions

1. Preheat smoker to 225°F (110°C).
2. Mix maple syrup, mustard, and black pepper, then brush over sausages.
3. Smoke for 2 hours, turning occasionally.

BBQ S'mores with Maple Graham Crackers

Ingredients

- 8 maple-flavored graham crackers
- 4 marshmallows
- 4 squares dark chocolate

Instructions

1. Preheat grill to medium-low heat.
2. Toast marshmallows over the grill.
3. Sandwich chocolate and marshmallows between maple graham crackers.

Smoked Arctic Char Tacos

Ingredients

- 2 Arctic char fillets
- 1 tbsp olive oil
- 1 tsp smoked paprika
- 1/2 tsp salt
- 1/4 tsp black pepper
- 6 small tortillas

Toppings

- 1/2 cup shredded cabbage
- 2 tbsp lime juice
- 1 tbsp maple syrup
- 1/4 cup sour cream

Instructions

1. Preheat smoker to 225°F (110°C).
2. Rub Arctic char with olive oil, paprika, salt, and pepper.
3. Smoke for 1 hour, then flake into tacos.
4. Toss cabbage with lime juice and maple syrup.
5. Serve tacos with cabbage and sour cream.

Grilled Sweet Potatoes with Maple Butter

Ingredients

- 2 large sweet potatoes, sliced
- 2 tbsp olive oil
- 1/4 cup maple syrup
- 2 tbsp butter, melted
- 1/2 tsp cinnamon
- 1/2 tsp salt

Instructions

1. Preheat grill to medium heat.
2. Toss sweet potato slices with olive oil and salt.
3. Grill for 3-4 minutes per side.
4. Mix maple syrup, butter, and cinnamon, then drizzle over sweet potatoes before serving.

BBQ Pulled Moose Sliders

Ingredients

- 2 lbs moose roast
- 1/2 cup maple BBQ sauce
- 1/2 cup beef broth
- 1 tbsp apple cider vinegar
- 1 tsp garlic powder
- 1/2 tsp black pepper
- 12 slider buns

Instructions

1. Place moose roast in a slow cooker with BBQ sauce, broth, vinegar, garlic powder, and pepper.
2. Cook on low for 6-8 hours until tender.
3. Shred moose and serve on slider buns.